That your petitioner acquired _his_ claim to the aforesaid service or labor of said _eleven persons,_ in manner following: (2) _Lettie Howard and her child Tilly were purchased from Peter Havenner some 8 or 9 years ago, for eight hundred dollars, and her five other children were born since. — Levi Thomas and his wife Rachel, he purchased in Baltimore about the same time, and paid nine hundred and fifty dollars for them: — Ann Ross he acquired by his wife: — and Philip Reid he purchased in Charleston, S. C. many years ago when he was quite a youth. He bought him because of his evident talent for the ~~foundry~~ business in which your petitioner was engaged, and paid twelve hundred dollars for him. — His papers having been burnt some years ago, he has no record evidence of his title._

That your petitioner's claim to the service or labor of said _eleven persons_ was, at the time of said discharge therefrom, of the value of _(see below)_ dollars in money. (3) _Lettie Howard, — seven hundred dollars_ $700.00

(see preceding page.)

Tilly Howard,	_five hundred dollars_	500.00
Tom Howard,	_five hundred dollars_	500.00
Ellick Howard,	_four hundred dollars_	400.00
Jackson Howard,	_two hundred & fifty dollars_	250.00
George Howard,	_one hundred & fifty dollars_	150.00
Emily Howard,	_fifty dollars_	50.00
Levi Thomas,	_three hundred dollars_	300.00
Rachel Thomas,	_four hundred dollars_	400.00
Ann Ross	_five hundred dollars ($500.—)_	500.00
Philip Reid,	_fifteen hundred dollars_	1,500.00
		5,250.00

Your petitioner hereby declares that _he_ bears true and faithful allegiance to the Government of the United States, and that _he_ has not borne arms against the United States in the present rebellion, nor in any way given aid or comfort thereto.

And your petitioner further states and alleges, that _he_ has not brought said _eleven persons_ into the District of Columbia since the passage of said act of Congress; and that, at the time of the passage thereof, said _eleven persons were_ ~~was~~ held to service or labor therein under and by virtue of your petitioner's claim to such service or labor.

Your petitioner further states and alleges, that _his_ said claim to the service or labor of said _eleven persons,_ does not originate in or by virtue of any transfer heretofore made by any person who has in any manner aided or sustained the present rebellion against the Government of the United States.

And your petitioner prays the said Commissioners to investigate and determine the validity of _his_ said claim to the service or labor of said _eleven persons_ herein above set forth; and if the same be found to be valid, that they appraise and apportion the value of said claim in money, and report the same to the Secretary of the Treasury of the United States, in conformity to the provisions of said act of Congress.

(Signed by)

Clark Mills

Note (1.)—Here describe the person, so as to identify him or her; and if there be more than one slave, describe each one separately.

Note (2.)—Here state how the claim was acquired, when, from whom, and for what price or consideration; and, if held under any written evidence of title, make exhibit thereof, or refer to the public record where the same may be found.

Note (3.)—Here state such facts, if any there be, touching the value of the petitioner's claim to the service or labor of the person, as may enhance the same, and also such facts, if any, touching the moral, mental, and bodily infirmities or defects of said person, as impair the value of the petitioner's claim to such service or labor, and conclude such statement with an averment that the petitioner knows of no other infirmities or defects of said person which impair the value of petitioner's claim to such service or labor, and that he believes none other to exist. If the petitioner specify no such infirmity or defect, then his statement touching the value of his claim should conclude with an averment that he has no knowledge of any such infirmity or defect.

To William C. Allen, former architectural historian for the Architect of the Capitol in Washington, D.C.;
and to Eleanor Holmes Norton, delegate to the U.S. Congress for the District of Columbia.
–E.W.

To Loretta Carter Hanes, an advocate for educating children about Emancipation Day, April 16, 1862,
in the city of Washington, D.C.; and to John A. Stokes, a lifelong elementary school educator
and a young leader of the 1951 high school student strike in Prince Edward County, Virginia.
–S.S.L.

For Patricia "Tish" Curtis. Thank you, I could not have survived Georgia without you.
–R.G.C.

The authors would like to acknowledge the following:
Individuals
Felicia Bell, Savannah State University, Savannah, Georgia
John Philip Colletta, Historian, Washington, D.C.
Leslie T. Fenwick, Howard University, Washington, D.C.
C. R. Gibbs, Historian of the African Diaspora, Washington, D.C.
Peter Hanes, Editor and Historian, Washington, D.C.
Michael Shapiro, Director, High Museum of Art, Atlanta, Georgia
Carol Swann-Wright, Monticello, Charlottesville, Virginia
David Taft Terry, University of Maryland, College Park, Maryland

Institutions (in Washington, D.C., unless otherwise stated)
Architect of the Capitol
California Foundry Museum, El Dorado Hills, California
Historical Society of Washington, D.C.
Howard University
Library of Congress
Middleton Place, Charleston, South Carolina
National Archives and Records Administration
National Council for the Social Studies, Silver Spring, Maryland
National Museum of African American History and Culture
National Museum of American History
Reginald F. Lewis Museum of Maryland African American History & Culture, Baltimore
United States Capitol Historical Society
United States Census Bureau
White House Historical Association

Text Copyright © 2014 Steven Sellers Lapham and Eugene Walton
Illustration Copyright © 2014 R. Gregory Christie

Sleeping Bear Press™

315 E. Eisenhower Pkwy., Suite 200
Ann Arbor, MI 48108
www.sleepingbearpress.com

Printed and bound in the United States.
10 9 8 7 6 5 4 3 2

Library of Congress Cataloging-in-Publication Data • Lapham, Steven Sellers, author. • Philip Reid saves the statue of freedom • Written by Steven Sellers Lapham and Dr. Eugene Walton ; Illustrated by R. Gregory Christie. • pages cm • ISBN 978-1-58536-819-8 • 1. Reid, Philip, approximately 1820---Anecdotes--Juvenile literature. • 2. Crawford, Thomas, 1813 or 14-1857. Freedom--Anecdotes--Juvenile • literature. 3. Foundry workers--United States--Anecdotes--Juvenile • literature. 4. African Americans--Anecdotes--Juvenile literature. I. • Walton, Eugene, author. II. Christie, R. Gregory, 1971- illustrator. III. • Title. • E340.R45L37 2013 • 973'.0496073--dc23 • 2013002586

PHILIP REID
Saves the
STATUE of FREEDOM

Steven Sellers Lapham & Eugene Walton

Illustrated by R. Gregory Christie

PUBLISHED BY SLEEPING BEAR PRESS

*P*hilip learned how things work from Jim, an old man. Jim showed young Philip how clay softens as you add water and work it with your hands. How wax and metal soften with heat. How wood cuts more easily after it has dried for a year in the sun.

Jim learned these things as a boy in West Africa, where Yoruba artisans were famous for their skill in casting brass statuettes and fancy gold jewelry.

Jim was now enslaved in the United States. Philip was born into American slavery before the Civil War.

Philip learned about people from his mother, Betsy. One day, when he was ten years old, she said,

"We are enslaved. But even so, there is a moment for speaking the truth." Betsy also advised him,

"Be patient. On this Earth, all things change. One day, slavery will end. Then you will be a free man."

Philip lived on a plantation near Charleston, South Carolina. He worked with the craftsmen who did jobs in the big yard. He pumped the bellows for the blacksmith. He stoked the kiln when the potter fired clay jugs. As he worked, he watched and learned.

One day, a craftsman named Clark Mills came to create fancy plaster molding on the walls and ceilings of the master's home. Philip was excited to help Mr. Mills mix the plaster, and he held the ladder steady as Mills worked.

When the week ended, Mills told Philip's master, "I need a skilled slave to be my assistant. What price would you ask for Philip?"

When Philip left with Mr. Mills, Philip's mother knew she might never see her son again.

Clark Mills moved to Washington, D.C., where he became a famous sculptor. In Mills's foundry, Philip helped to cast large objects in bronze. There were many steps in the process. Philip became skilled at repairing breaks in the plaster models and making the molds that would hold the liquid bronze.

It was always exciting when the day arrived for foundry workers to pour hot, molten bronze into the mold to create the statue. Philip was in charge of controlling the fire to melt the copper and tin, metals that make bronze.

"The pour" was a dangerous and magical moment. Any flaw in the materials, any mistake in the movements of the workers, could cause an accident. The liquid bronze glowed with its own inner light. It moved like an orange tiger as it flowed into the mold.

The United States government hired Mills to cast a statue called *Freedom* in bronze. It would stand atop the new dome of the Capitol in Washington, D.C. One day in 1859, Clark Mills and Philip Reid traveled to the Capitol to fetch the plaster model for the statue *Freedom.* Four wagons were filled with straw to cushion the five large sections of the model.

Mills and Reid entered the room where the plaster model was on exhibit. It was framed by a scaffold. But something was wrong. About ten men were gathered around the plaster model of the statue, looking at it and talking.

An Italian craftsman had put the five big sections of the plaster model together. He covered up the seams with plaster, and now nobody could see where the seams were. The craftsman would not tell how to take the model apart for transport to the foundry. He wanted more money to finish the job.

"Only I can do it," the craftsman asserted. "If you try, it will break."

How could anybody else find the places where the five sections of the plaster model fit together? The seams were hidden with white plaster, just like icing hides the layers of a cake.

None of the other men in the room could solve the problem. Or, they were afraid. If they made a wrong move, the plaster model might crack badly. If that happened, thousands of dollars would be wasted. The Capitol dome might not have a statue at its peak for many years.

There was an uneasy silence in the room. Clark Mills stepped forward and said,

"My assistant, Philip Reid, can solve this puzzle."

The chief engineer looked doubtfully at Philip.

"Can you do this?" he asked.

Philip quickly studied the problem. Then he turned to the engineer and said,

"Yes, I believe that I can."

Philip knew a lot about plaster from his years of experience working in the foundry. He knew how much force it takes to break it, and how to keep it from breaking.

Phillip worked slowly and carefully. He climbed to the top of the scaffold. He told the workers below to pull carefully on the ropes. Ropes and pulleys were attached to an iron hook embedded in the top of the statue.

"Pull one arm's length," he said, "and then hold the rope steady. Ready? Heave . . . ho!"

The workers pulled, but there was no sign of a seam in the plaster mold.

Philip called again, "Heave . . . ho!"

The workers pulled another arm's length of rope. The rope strained—and suddenly, yes! Philip noticed something. There was a seam running along the top of the shoulders.

Now Philip could see where the top section was attached to the section below it. He could also see the faint outline of the flat, round head of a bolt. Using a tool, he loosened and removed it. Then he moved to the next bolt along the linear seam and removed it. Then the next. Philip had to work slowly.

Everybody watched, but nobody asked him what he was doing. Philip was already earning their respect.

Finally, all of the bolts were removed.
All that was needed was a bit more
upward force.

"This time, pull two arms' lengths,"
Philip said to the workmen.

"Heave . . . ho! Heave . . . ho!"

The men handling the ropes pulled.
Suddenly the top section–head, neck,
and shoulders–lifted cleanly away.
The onlookers gasped.

Philip peered inside the plaster model. Looking down, he could see the next row of bolts. One by one, he loosened and removed those bolts. Section by section, he worked. In less than an hour, five plaster sections sat separately side by side on the floor. Philip Reid had solved the puzzle.

Everyone in the room sensed that something special had happened. The Italian craftsman left the room angrily. Everyone else was glad that the plaster model had not broken. Philip Reid had discovered how to take the plaster model apart. The work could go on.

Philip was very pleased with his accomplishment. He remembered the words of his mother and Jim, encouraging him every step of the way. Looking over the five sections of the model lying side by side on the floor, Philip knew in his heart that he had just achieved a high goal, and he felt grateful.

It took two years to create the bronze
Statue of Freedom. Philip controlled
the fires in the foundry. The work
continued, even on Sundays, when
everybody—slaves and masters—usually
rested. The United States government
paid Philip for his work on Sundays
during the casting of *Freedom.* For
Philip, this was a taste of the true
freedom to come. The Civil War had
started. Freedom seemed just around
the corner for Philip and all enslaved
Americans. And it was!

Epilogue

Philip Reid was freed in accordance with the District of Columbia Emancipation Act on April 16, 1862. Passage of this law came eight and a half months before President Lincoln issued his Emancipation Proclamation. Philip worked as a plasterer, and he had a wife and a son, according to U.S. Census records of 1870 and 1880. He was "in business for himself, and highly esteemed by all who knew him," said Fisk Mills, the son of foundry owner Clark Mills, in 1869.

Philip passed away on February 6, 1892, according to his death certificate. His remains are probably among the unmarked graves at Harmony Memorial Park Cemetery in Landover, Maryland.

We don't know if Philip Reid witnessed the event, but he was a free man when the last piece of the *Statue of Freedom* was put into place atop the Capitol dome on December 2, 1863. On that day, he would have heard a 35-gun salute, which was answered by the guns of the twelve forts around Washington. Today *Freedom* is seen up close only by birds as they wing over the U.S. Capitol in Washington, D.C.

And what about the plaster model of *Freedom*? Thomas Crawford, who designed the statue, created the model in Rome, Italy. After surviving mishaps at sea, the model's five sections arrived in Washington, D.C. in 1859. They were used in Clark Mills's foundry in the casting of the bronze statue. Today the plaster model of *Freedom* stands in the Capitol Visitor Center where visitors can view it up close.

Authors' Note

To create the story of Philip Reid as a child, we used historical evidence of what life was like for many enslaved Americans at that time. For example, we do not know the name of Philip's mother or who taught him crafts. We have no drawing or photo of Philip. But we do know that enslaved African Americans worked as skilled blacksmiths, carpenters, cooks, potters, and weavers on large plantations. Enslaved children typically began performing simple tasks at age six or seven. If a child was being trained for a craft, he or she might begin an apprenticeship at age ten, or soon after.

On July 7, 2009, the U.S. House of Representatives passed a resolution honoring the contributions of African Americans in building the U.S. Capitol. Resolution 135 describes how Philip Reid "deciphered the puzzle of how to separate the 5-piece plaster model for casting when all others failed." With these words, Congress helped correct the record of U.S. history, in which the role of African Americans has too often been suppressed and erased.

Philip Reid's pay stub records some of his work in the bronze foundry. He was paid $1.25 per day. The U.S. government paid him for his work on Sundays, typically considered a day of rest.

Note about document on end sheets:

The PETITION of 1862 printed in the front and back of this book was created as a way for a slave owner, such as Clark Mills, to receive payment from the U.S. government when slavery ended in the District of Columbia in 1862. Slaves were not compensated for their years in bondage. This document provides the best description we have today of Philip Reid. Mills was required to briefly describe each of his slaves and list his or her "value" in dollars. Philip Reid is cited as the most valuable person on the list, "worth" $1,500. However, the government limited payment to $300 for each person. The name "Philip Reid" appears four times in the document.

PETITION.

Your Petitioner, *Clark Mills* of *Washington County D.C.* by this *his* petition in writing, represents and states, that *he* is a person loyal to the United States, who, at the time of the passage of the said act of Congress, held a claim to service or labor against

six male and five female

person*s* of African descent of the name*s* of *Lettie Howard and her children Tilly, Tom, Elick, Jackson, George and Emily; — Levi Thomas, Rachel Thomas, Ann Ross, and Philip Reid,*

for and during the life*s* of said *eleven persons,*

and that by said act of Congress said *eleven persons*

were discharged and freed of and from all claim of your petitioner to such service or labor; that at the time of said discharge said *eleven persons*

were of the age*s* of

and of the personal description following: [1] viz: — *Lettie Howard, 33 years old, color black; short and thick set — healthy; — her six children, Tilly, 10 years, Tom, 8 years, — Elick, 6½ years, — Jackson, 5 years, — George, 3 years, — and Emily, 3 months old, all black color, sound and healthy; — Levi Thomas, 59 years old, black color, over six feet high, a large leg rather stiff, but sound and in good health; — Rachel Thomas, his wife, 49 years old, mullatto color, healthy, very large, weighs about 200 pounds; Ann Ross, 48 years, mullatto color, about five feet seven inches high, rather slim make, and in good health; — and Philip Reid, aged 42 years, mullatto color, short in stature, in good health, not prepossessing in appearance, but smart in mind, a good workman in a foundry, and has been employed in that capacity by the Government, at one dollar and twenty five cents per day. — Your Petitioner is not aware that any of above possess any moral, mental, or bodily infirmities that impair their value; and does not believe that any such exist; except that mentioned in regard to the stiff leg of Levi Thomas. —*